Leeds

Leeds

Paul Barker

FRANCES LINCOLN LIMITED
PUBLISHERS

ABOVE, LEFT TO RIGHT
Leeds United Football Club, Elland Road;
Tetley's Brewery, Waterloo Street;
Wash day, Marley Grove, Holbeck;
Chapeltown allotment

Frances Lincoln Ltd
4 Torriano Mews
Torriano Avenue
London NW5 2RZ
www.franceslincoln.com

First Frances Lincoln edition 2010

A catalogue record for this book is available from the British
Library.

ISBN 978-0-7112-2920-4

Printed and bound in Singapore

acknowledgments

I would like to thank the following people and organizations
for their help during the making of this book: Christopher H.L.
Tyne, Trevor Parker, Dan Woodward, The Churches Conser-
vation Trust, Father A.T. Myers, Steven Savage, Reverend Tim
Gill, Reverend David Stephens, Karen Smales, Nicola Hanson,
Darren Beard, Sarah Stiller, Jane Verity, Andrea Wadsworth,
Ian Fime, Alex Dalton, James Butler, Andy Bonner, Morgans
Plus, Country Life, The Management Team at Leeds Town
Hall. I would also like to thank Chris Ireland and Phase One for
all their technical assistance.

dedication

I would like to dedicate this book to the people of Leeds
without whose help, co-operation and friendliness a book such
as this would not be possible.

contents

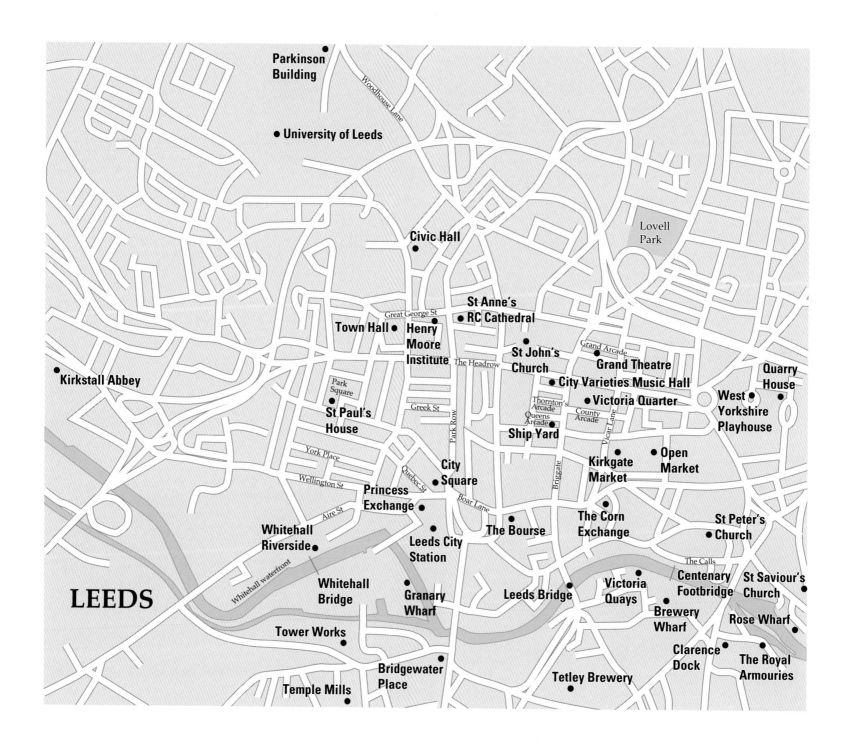

Parkinson Building

University of Leeds

Woodhouse Lane

Civic Hall

Lovell Park

St Anne's
RC Cathedral

Great George St

Town Hall

Henry Moore Institute

St John's Church

Grand Arcade

Grand Theatre

City Varieties Music Hall

The Headrow

Victoria Quarter

Quarry House

West Yorkshire Playhouse

Kirkstall Abbey

Park Square

St Paul's House

Greek St

Thornton's Arcade

Queens Arcade

County Arcade

Ship Yard

York Place

Park Row

City Square

Kirkgate Market

Open Market

Wellington St

Quebec St

Briggate

Vicar Lane

Aire St

Princess Exchange

Boar Lane

The Bourse

The Corn Exchange

St Peter's Church

Whitehall Riverside

Leeds City Station

Whitehall waterfront

The Calls

Centenary Footbridge

St Saviour's Church

LEEDS

Whitehall Bridge

Granary Wharf

Leeds Bridge

Victoria Quays

Brewery Wharf

Rose Wharf

Tower Works

Clarence Dock

Bridgewater Place

Tetley Brewery

The Royal Armouries

Temple Mills

introduction

Over the past decade Leeds has become an extremely busy and successful city. If you are returning here after a long absence, it is quite possible that it has changed almost beyond recognition. From rejuvenation to restoration and from demolition to new build, Leeds has seen it all. Those magnificent Victorian buildings, such as the Town Hall, the Corn Exchange and the wonderful warehouses, now look so much happier among the likes of Clarence Dock and Bridgewater Place. The mix looks right. The restorations of the Victoria Quarter have brought a new kind of shop to suit the needs of a new breed of shopper. It may be the beginning of the twenty-first century, but Leeds seems to be enjoying the kind of success it hasn't seen for the last 150 years. Long may it last; it hasn't been an easy ride.

ABOVE
Leeds Town Hall

RIGHT
The Corn Exchange

Temple Newsam House

history

The central part of Leeds has been occupied since the Middle Ages. Very little evidence survives today, but over the centuries there have been archaeological finds that give us an insight into the early history of Leeds.

Evidence of settlements in the region of Leeds during the Bronze and Iron Ages has been found near to present-day Briggate and at Roundhay. Prehistoric defensive sites dating from around 1500 BC have been found at Chapel Allerton, Woodhouse Moor, Temple Newsam and Quarry Hill. It is believed that during Roman times Leeds was a place of some importance, as it was situated at the meeting of a number of Roman roads. There were many Roman settlements and forts throughout Yorkshire and several on the roads connecting them to larger settlements. For example, Adel, just to the north of the city, lies on the road from York to Ilkley, and a large quantity of Roman artifacts has been found found here. On the road between York and Manchester there were the settlements of Tadcaster and Cambodunum. Although the present-day location of the latter is not known, it is thought that the name Cambodunum means 'the fort by the river bend', and archaeologists in more recent times have begun to believe that the site of Cambodunum may in fact have been Leeds. In 1715 evidence was found of a very large camp at Quarry Hill, but it is not clear whether this was a Roman or Saxon site. In 1819, on a site near to Leeds Bridge, workmen discovered evidence of a Roman fort and road along with coins and pottery.

After the Romans left Britain, the country was divided into small kingdoms and the area where Leeds is situated now was in the kingdom of Elmet. In AD 617 Edwin, the Anglo-Saxon king of Northumbria, conquered the area and expelled its king, Ceretic. The name of Leeds probably came into being at this time, Loidis meaning 'the people living by the river', and later Leedis.

Substantial remains of five memorial crosses dating from the ninth and tenth centuries, discovered at Leeds Parish Church in 1838, are evidence that Leeds was an important early settlement. No doubt these prominent individuals of means had thought the site to be of sufficient importance to choose it as a place of burial.

There is very little evidence as to how the area of present-day Leeds was divided before the Norman Conquest. In the Domesday survey, the manor of Leeds was recorded along with smaller manors now more familiar as the suburbs of the city, such as Allerton, Hunslett, Holbeck and Headingley. Much of the woodland around those parts had been used for building and burning during medieval times. Only two major areas of woodland remained, plus one area of common land where all tenants could graze their cattle: Woodhouse Moor.

William the Conqueror had vested the manor of Leeds to Ilbert de Lacy, who in 1086 granted it to Ralph Paynel (Paganel), a wealthy Norman baron who set about a period of stripping the main assets from the corn mills and parts of the land. In 1089 the extensive manor was broken up and Leeds parish church, its income and the surrounding villages and land, were given by Paynel to the Holy Trinity Priory at York and was administrated from a separate manor house in The

Calls. The Knights Templar were also given small parcels of land and in 1155 acquired the manor of Newsam.

Maurice de Gant, a descendant of Paynel, gained possession of the manor of Leeds around 1200. It was in a poor state and he soon realised that radical action was needed if the manor was ever going to provide him with an income. He decided to divide the manor into boroughs, the result of which was to allow the inhabitants the freedom to move around and hopefully encourage skilled craftsmen to come into the village and settle. In 1207 Maurice granted a charter creating the borough of Leeds, the new town extending from the river crossing at Leeds Bridge and Kirkgate to the open fields of Woodhouse Moor. Thirty plots were marked out on either side of a new street. These were called Burgate plots and the people living there were called Burgesses. This street was later to be called Briggate. The new inhabitants were also given half-acre plots of land at Burma Tofts (Burgage Men's Tofts) now Burmantofts. They were to earn their living not from agriculture but from a trade and were charged an annual rent of 16d. At first it was not a great success, but it was of major significance as it set the pattern of Leeds. Briggate was soon to become the main street in the village and its layout is still very much in evidence today.

Throughout the thirteenth and fourteenth centuries the majority of people in the borough were living off the land, relying heavily on the success of the harvest and the grazing of sheep and cattle. The communities were largely self-supporting; besides farming there were a number of skilled craftsmen such as carpenters and blacksmiths. Maurice de Gant's founding of a more commercial centre around Briggate was beginning to bear fruit by the middle of the thirteenth century. By the turn of the century markets and fairs were being held, each bringing

Kirkstall Abbey

Leeds Bridge

into the manor a range of goods that were not normally available locally. It was around this time that a new industry began to grow, which was to prove pivotal in shaping the history of Leeds – the making of woollen cloth.

The softness of the water from the River Aire played a vital part in the success of the cloth finishing process. Initially the woollen industry was slow to start, as it was dominated by towns such as York and Beverley. However, Leeds had a supply of good wool from the sheep which had been introduced by the Cistercian monks of Kirkstall.

During the making of woollen cloth there was a very labour-intensive process known as fulling, which gave the cloth after weaving a smooth, softer finish and had the advantage of making it more hard wearing. This process involved soaking the cloth in a mixture of water, urine and full-ers earth, and it was then pounded to knit the fibres together. It required a team of twelve people to achieve this, but with the invention of water-powered fulling mills the pounding of the cloth became less arduous. There were not many fulling mills as they were very expensive to build, but they were very profitable. By 1322 on the east side of Leeds Bridge a fulling mill was built by the lord of the manor, which greatly encouraged the growth of the cloth industry. Other specialist workers involved in the making of wool were attracted to the area, such as dyers. By 1356 a second mill was built, this

time on the west side of the river and by the end of the fourteenth century the woollen industry was beginning to bring great prosperity to the manor. The manor had at this time been passed from Maurice de Gant to Henry of Lancaster, making Leeds the property of the Crown when he became King Henry IV in 1399.

By 1500 it was still agriculture that dominated life in the manor, but the two previous centuries had seen a huge growth in the woollen cloth industry. Clothiers were producing cloth in their cottages in rural hamlets and in the town. The now-bustling market town drew in large numbers, attracted by low rents and woollen manufacturing facilities.

Elizabethan Leeds saw even greater growth and the clothiers became increasingly more successful. After the dissolution of Kirkstall Abbey in 1539, land flooded on to the market, much of it bought by yeomen farmers and clothiers. This also attracted people to Leeds from elsewhere, bringing with them a considerable change to the agricultural framework. Such large numbers of people placed new demands on the land. The traditional open strips of land had been made into long narrow fields surrounded by walls and hedges and by 1548 all remaining land had been enclosed, bringing to an end all communal farming. The town was beginning to outgrow its manorial framework. The population of Leeds grew rapidly, doubling in size to 4,000 by 1600.

St John the Evangelist, New Briggate

Throughout the fourteenth and fifteenth centuries the local gentry had held manorial offices, but by the sixteenth century it was the wealthier clothiers and tradesmen who sought to control the town and its industry. In 1570 the first attempt to secure a charter creating a corporation in Leeds failed. It was an idea of good intention. The real concern was to ensure a kind of quality control and that the name of Leeds cloth stood for true quality: anyone not sticking to the guidelines would be prosecuted. However on 26 July 1626 Charles I did incorporate Leeds, thereby giving the town powers of self-government.

The woollen cloth industry, on which the wealth of Leeds was based in the seventeenth century, was a very important industry for other parts of the country as well, notably the West Country, East Anglia and other parts of the West Riding, all producing their own particular kind of cloth. The area around Leeds specialized in a coarse cloth known as Yorkshire Broad-

cloths or Northern Dozens. One reason Leeds enjoyed such great success was its being situated at a major crossing point of the river on the main route from Chester to York. The other cloth-producing areas in the West Riding brought their goods to market in Leeds, which made Leeds not only a principal cloth market and finishing centre but also a funnel through which food and all other necessities of life passed. Though smaller and less important than Halifax and Wakefield as a textile centre in the previous century, Leeds had now outgrown them both.

The seventeenth century saw a great improvement in the way houses were built. Once made of oak, wattle and daub with thatched roofs, stone and brick buildings with slate and tiled roofs became popular. The important houses at that time were built in the newly fashionable areas of Boar Lane, and the Headrow. The town's amenities also greatly improved, a

Briggate

new Moot Hall was built in 1615, a new grammar school in 1624 and St John's Church in 1631–4. Life for the wealthy was good.

However, unsettling events were unfolding that were to have a profound effect on the history of Leeds as they did on many other parts of the country. The first was on 22 August 1642 when, Charles I raised the standard in Nottingham. His dispute with Parliament had become the English Civil War. There were conflicting views in Leeds, and tension existed between the merchants and the clothiers, the merchants generally speaking backing the Royalist cause. Leeds, now a prosperous market town, was in the thick of the conflict. There were many battles, with each side trying to gain control over Leeds and other major Yorkshire towns. Success went from one side to the other. First the Royalist got the upper hand then the Parliamentarians and by April 1643 Leeds was virtually under

siege. This exchange continued until 7 April 1644, when Sir Thomas Fairfax managed to retake the town. From that date the town remained under the control of the Parliamentarians. The entire county of Yorkshire went the same way later that year after the Battle of Marston Moor. The financial demands of the occupying armies, the loss of life and damage to property resulted in Leeds suffering badly in the Civil War.

If that were not enough, there was another blow about to hit the people of Leeds. Throughout the first half of the seventeenth century England was rarely without the bubonic plague. Black rats carrying the fleas whose bite transmitted the disease were brought by trading ships. The very first victim in Leeds is believed to have been Alice Musgrave of Vicar Lane, who died in March 1645. The disease seemed to affect the poor more, and their cramped and over crowded living conditions around Vicar Lane, The Calls and the lower part of Briggate appeared

to fuel the disease. A vigil was kept and as soon as a family was suspected of having the disease, all members of the household were removed to specially built cabins on Quarry Hill, later to be known as 'Cabin Closes'. They were watched over and fed, but were not allowed to leave the cabins. All the while their houses remained locked up and empty. Markets in the town were suspended and transferred to Woodhouse Moor, to which corn, cloth and other commodities could only be brought by those traders who held a certificate declaring their goods free from disease. The wealthier families abandoned the town and moved to the country and it is believed that there were very few if not any deaths among the upper classes. However in that short period of time from March to December 1645 it is believed that more than 1,325 people died in Leeds from the plague, about one fifth of the population. The first half of the seventeenth century had been a truly testing time not only for the people of Leeds, but throughout the country. The Civil War had caused great physical damage to the town, and the plague greatly reduced its population. It is a true testament to the resilience and character of the people of Leeds that they were able to bounce back from these two great shocks and resume its path to even greater prosperity.

OPPOSITE AND BELOW
Park Row

Briggate had become lined with a variety of dwellings — fine mansion houses often mingling with more humble timber-framed buildings. It was a focal point of commercial activity with many shops, offices and workshops. In the eighteenth century Briggate, Vicar Lane, Kirkgate and the Headrow retained much of their medieval street pattern. The population between 1700 and 1771 had increased from 6,000 to 16,500. Physically the built-up area did not increase so one can only presume that conditions became very overcrowded. By 1781 Leeds was growing at its most rapid: in 1773 there were 3,347 houses and by 1793 there were 6,691. Amazingly by the 1790s the population had increased to 25,000.

The phenomenal growth of the wool industry in the eighteenth century brought along with it many other crafts and trades, which became important in their own right. Leeds had become the commercial capital of the West Riding. The fact that the town was surrounded by coalmines attracted other manufacturing industries, especially in the latter part of the century, such as brick makers (to supply the huge need of house building), potters and soap boilers. Housing for the lower classes was crammed into every available yard, garden or patch of land in close proximity to the main streets. Some of the wealthier merchants began moving out to finer houses in the more fashionable areas, such as Park Row. Often their abandoned houses were divided up into smaller places for both residential and commercial use.

Leeds had become surrounded by other cloth-making towns. While Leeds specialized in coloured or broad cloth that had already been dyed, other districts around Huddersfield and Bradford specialized in white or undyed broad cloth. In these districts lived huge numbers of clothiers, who worked in their own homes. The cloth they produced more often than not

Botany Bay

went to market in Leeds. Cloth merchant and clothiers met at cloth markets, which by the middle of the eighteenth century were still held in Briggate on Tuesdays and Saturdays. Wares were sold from trestle tables that lined the street often two deep on both sides. It was usual for merchants to come to Leeds to buy broad cloth just as it was for Leeds merchants to go elsewhere to buy narrow cloths and worsteds.

A threat to the prosperity of the merchants of Leeds came in the early eighteenth century, when merchants in Wakefield built their own cloth hall in a bid to attract merchants away from Leeds. Leeds merchants were quick to respond and in 1711 a White Cloth Hall was built in Kirkgate. Trade expanded at such a rate that by 1756 a new and bigger White Cloth Hall was built south of the river in Meadow Lane. At the same time a massive Coloured Cloth Hall was built on a site where City Square stands today. It was the largest hall in Leeds, measur-

ing 127 yards long and 66 yards wide, and it was financed by the clothiers themselves at a cost of £5,300; sadly it was demolished in 1890. Yet another White Cloth Hall was built in 1776 between The Calls and Kirkgate. Regrettably, very little evidence of these very fine and historic buildings remains today.

The town was growing fast and transport was of great importance. Many roads were just tracks, often turning to mud in wet weather. In the 1740s turnpikes were introduced and the money earned from the tolls was used to improve and repair the roads. As only to be expected, the tolls proved to be very unpopular with the people who had to pay them, and riots erupted, the worst of which was in 1753 at The King's Arms in Briggate, where a troop of dragoons had to be called out in order to keep the peace. Shots were fired and a number of people were killed.

Rose Wharf and St Saviour's Church

Leeds was one of the first towns to experience the Industrial Revolution; the glorious Georgian era was coming to an end and the charms of Leeds began to be destroyed with the arrival of factories whose chimneys belched out thick smoke. In many ways Leeds would never be the same again.

The beginning of the Industrial Revolution saw the rise of the Luddite movement. Factory building had begun in earnest and woollen mills sprang up all over Leeds. Attempts had been made to introduce machinery that would do the cloth work previously carried out by proud, highly skilled and respected craftsmen. These craftsmen now feared that their finely tuned craft would become the work of mere factory hands. Those who feared most for their jobs were the croppers and cloth dressers, whose skill was to raise the nap of the cloth, trim it and then press it. Skirmishes and outbreaks of violence erupted throughout the West Riding, but more particularly in Leeds and Huddersfield where the Luddites destroyed the machinery and set the mills alight. A particularly nasty incident occurred at Rawfolds Mill, owned by William Cartwright, in April 1812, when two people were killed. However none of this was to stop the painful reorganisation of the industry, which was gradually brought about by a large militia presence and well-publicised arrests. Perhaps a sad end to this saga is that in 1812 there had been 1,733 croppers in Leeds. By the time the dust had settled they were proved right – it was the demise of their honourable craft.

Benjamin Gott was possibly the first of the great Leeds entrepreneurs. He had served his apprenticeship as a gentleman merchant but became increasingly frustrated at his inability to obtain the super-fine cloth which was becoming very popular in America and which hitherto had been produced mainly in the West Country. To overcome this problem he decided to branch out into the manufacture of woollen cloth. Over the following decade he built mills at Bean Ing (later to become known as Park Mills) and later other mills in Armley and Burley. By 1820 Benjamin Gott had a work force of 1,200 people and was one of the largest employers in England. Not only did his mills manufacture the super-fine cloth, but he also brought it in from places outside Leeds, such as Huddersfield, whereupon he would finish and re-sell it. The quality of his cloth was beyond compare and produced in such large quantities that no other merchant had a hope of matching it. In addition to

ABOVE LEFT
Ashwood Terrace

LEFT
Back Grosvenor Terrace, Headingley

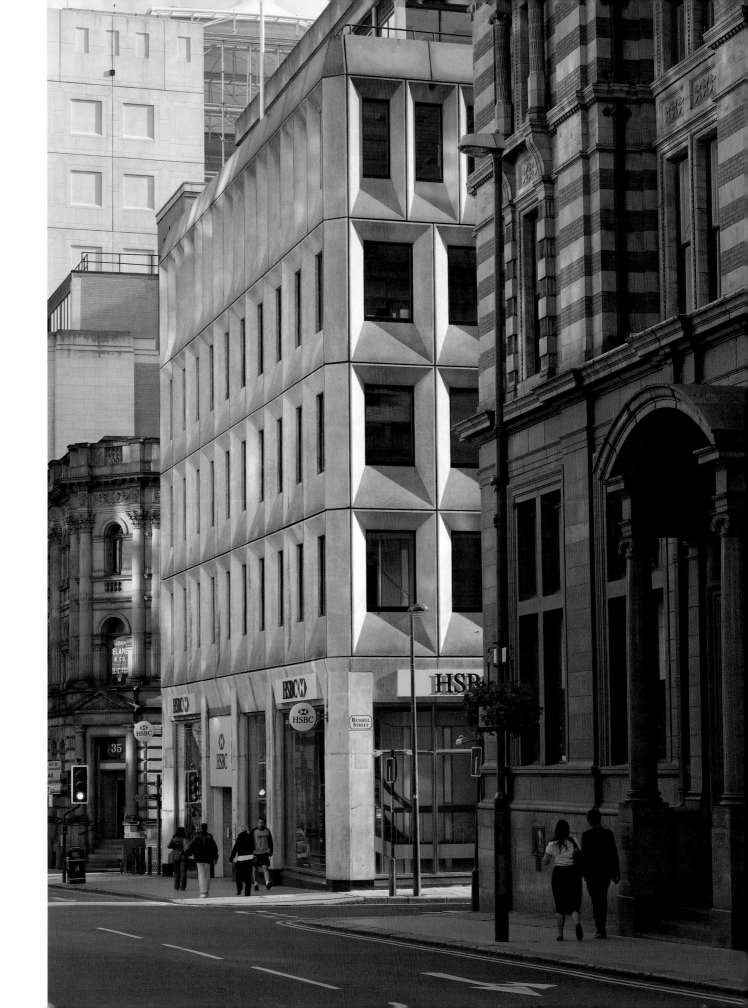

Park Row

super-fine, Gott also produced blankets and uniforms in vast numbers, selling them not only to the British Army but to other armies abroad. It soon became clear to others that there were large profits to be made and by 1822 in Leeds there were more than forty factories manufacturing woollen cloth.

It was not only the woollen industry that prevailed in Leeds at this time, but the cotton industry also. A leading figure here was John Marshall who, like Gott, made the most of his opportunity brought about during this period of Industrial Revolution. His field was cotton spinning. He abandoned water power for steam power to spin flax into linen yarn to produce heavy linen cloth such as canvas and hessian. Marshall employed 1,000 workers and there was no other flax spinner of such a size in the country. He was responsible, along with the much-travelled architect Joseph Bonomi, for building the remarkable Egyptian Revival Temple Mills in 1838–43, the design of which is based on the Temple of Horus at Edfu. Another great innovator at this time was a former employee of John Marshall, Matthew Murphy, who left to set up business in the manufacture of the machinery and utensils now much in demand in the new various industries growing in Leeds. His Round Foundry became famous for its production of textile machinery, steam engines and locomotives.

The growth of Leeds at this time was immense. As the population grew from 53,276 in 1801 to 152,000 in 1841, the face of Leeds had changed for ever. It was now one of the largest towns in England, dominated by factories and chimneys. It was believed that in 1842 there were about 175 factories in the region. Although the cloth industry prevailed, other indus-

tries were also taking hold, such as tailoring, dressmaking and the manufacture of shoes. Because of the growth in such diverse industries there was a huge demand for building. Leeds was now established as a major industrial centre. Transport links, so vital to maintain its position, were constantly improving. The inns and yards off Briggate and Boar Lane became highly sought after as commercial premises as the area developed into the coaching centre for the town, and by 1838 there were an astonishing 130 departures every day. Along with this came the need for accommodation, food and drinking establishments. Coal was another commoditity that Leeds consumed in vast quantities. It was believed that no town in England used more coal than Leeds. It can only be imagined what the quality of the air was like.

Until this point the most desirable places to live had been central. The more impressive houses in places such as Park Row and East Parade were owned by merchants and bankers, who now found themselves, as the population grew, living rather too close to those of 'lower rank'. The increase in noise and smoke brought about a change in fashion as large numbers moved out, building new houses and villas to the north of the town in places like Headingley.

There was also a growing need for low-cost housing in areas not too far from the town and places of work. Other towns had similar needs, but not on such a large scale as in Leeds. Some mill owners had built cottages or even entire villages to house their workers, but in Leeds this demand for housing was met by speculative building of large numbers of back-to-back houses that were usually rented out, mainly to the east

end of town around the Quarry Hill area, where an overall chaotic situation soon developed and the buildings were generally of poor quality. Certain areas saw dramatic changes. Kirkgate once a highly respected street, very near to the Parish Church soon became run down and dirty. Slightly further out, Holbeck, once a pleasant village surrounded by fields, soon became one of the most unpleasant and unhealthiest villages in the country.

It is true to say that the Victorian era left an indelible mark on the town, insofar as most of what we see today in Leeds comes from that very influential era, as it did in many northern towns and cities. In Leeds the Georgian era is still evident in the elegant squares such as Park Square but prior to that there is very little remaining apart from Kirkstall Abbey and a small number of churches. However, when it comes to the Victorian period, examples abound of public buildings, hotels, shop fronts, arcades, factories and warehouses. Most importantly it was in 1893 that Queen Victoria granted the charter designat-

ABOVE
St Paul's House, Park Square

ing Leeds a city. The wool industry was still going strong, but other industries were gaining ground, particularly engineering. Leeds was quite quickly becoming one of the world's engineering centres. Another industry that grew rapidly was the mass production of clothing. Clothes at that time had been made to the requirements of the individual by hand by a tailor or at home. John Barran, the son of a London gun maker, was about to change all this from a small factory off Boar Lane. On a visit to the 1851 Great Exhibition he had seen a band knife used to cut furniture veneers and he applied this same idea, which made it possible to cut many layers of woollen cloth at the same time. The factories also used the newly invented Singer sewing machines, which, along with the idea of keeping each employee to one task and making him or her particularly skilled at it, dramatically speeded the entire process. It was the beginning of a new industry that had the infrastructure already in place: a well-established transport system, local engineering skills and, most importantly, a workforce who

were used to handling cloth. Barran also dabbled in property development, particularly in areas such as Wellington Street, and in 1878 he commissioned Thomas Abler to build a new exotic Moorish style factory in Park Square. Today it houses offices and is known as St Paul's House.

Another major growth area in Leeds, as a result of the expansion in industry and commerce, was the the legal and financial services. The area that attracted this particular sector was Park Square; the same legal professions are still to be found in the very fine Georgian houses today. A number of banks and insurance companies were also established in the Park Row area along with, in 1846, the Leeds Stock Exchange, which was for many years the only stock exchange in a provincial town.

This wealth and the rising numbers of middle class citizens brought with it the desire for smart and elegant shops. The 1850s saw huge numbers of fine establishments selling everything that the elegant lady and gentleman about town should require, from furs and hats, boots and shoes to jewellery. Briggate, Commercial Street and Boar Lane were the places to be seen. (The same could be said today, as, wrongly or rightly, Leeds has gained the reputation of being the 'Knightsbridge of the North'.) One of the smartest shopping areas was the County Arcade and Cross Arcade, which were built in 1898–1903. They brought about a most spectacular transformation. In the middle of the nineteenth century it was in this very area,

between Briggate and Vicar Lane and around Kirkgate, that the other end of the social scale had lived and worked. It was an absolute warren of alleyways leading from one yard or square to another; here the line between sufficiency and poverty was very fine indeed. There was a mix of pubs, warehouses, shops, cottages, brothels and slaughterhouses. Sanitary conditions were not good, consisting of merely a gutter running down the middle of the alleys.

The nineteenth century saw many immigrants arriving in Leeds, first the Irish in the 1840s escaping the potato famine back home and arriving virtually penniless. Their attraction to the town had been the possibility of work in the woollen mills

Vicar Lane entrance to Victoria
Quarter

ABOVE
View from Beggars Hill

RIGHT
Burley Park railway station

Harehills

and warehouses. Of course many did find work and during the times of prosperity their labour was much in demand. However, many people in Leeds regarded them as anti-social and a major threat to public order. The next influx of immigrants were Jews fleeing the troubles in Russia in the 1880s. The clothing industry welcomed them with open arms. The wages paid to these immigrants was quite often very low, but the work was particularly suited to their skills and very soon many became highly successful tailors with reputations second to none. As with the Irish before them they were not always popular with everyone, due to nothing more than the way they dressed, a different language and the fact that for their own safety often lived together in their own commune.

Great steps were being taken by the council in the later part of the nineteenth century to provide a network of mains sewers, a fairly good water supply and an enormous amount of burial grounds. However what it was reluctant to do was to address the private housing problem, and they continued to ignore this right into the next century. The slum problem had hung around since the 1830s and it was still there in 1900. There had been no slum clearance policy. Purely by chance a few slums had been cleared when the Kirkgate Market had been built in 1850s, which had partly made the situation worse, as the council had provided no alternative accommodation; the people who were displaced had nowhere else to go but back to the remaining slums in the neighbourhood. No clear housing

policy was implemented, even when other towns in the country had banned the building of back-to-back houses.

As the population in Leeds had almost doubled between 1841 and 1901, so too had the number of houses, often built by speculative developers with no clear plan in mind. Areas such as Hunslett and Holbeck became dominated by back-to-back housing surrounding the mills and factories. With the arrival of the new century, the council embarked on a huge scheme of slum clearance. Sixty-seven acres of the worst slums in Leeds were cleared in the area around Quarry Hill and York Street and newer, stricter rules were laid down that all new housing had to be provided with WCs; at the same time major progress was made in the provision of sewers.

The later part of the Victorian era proved to be a period of significant development, both in the public and private sector. The magnificent Town Hall (1852–8), the Central Library (1872), the Grand Theatre (1878), the Municipal Buildings in Calverley Street (1884) and the Leeds Art Gallery (1888) all went to shape the city of Leeds that we see today.

The early part of the twentieth century saw a decrease in the population, partly due to the Great War of 1914–18 and

ABOVE LEFT
Reclining Woman (Elbow) and Central Library

ABOVE
Leeds Town Hall and Central Library

RIGHT
George Street

UNTIL THE DAY BREAK, AND THE SHADOWS FLEE AWAY.

SUSANNAH JANE,
WIFE OF JAMES AUDUS HIRST,
ADEL,
DIED FEBY 26TH 1884,
AGED 33 YEARS,
ALSO OF
JAMES AUDUS HIRST,
DIED SEPR 17TH 1896,
AGED 58 YEARS.

Monument of Susannah Audus,
St John the Baptist, Adel

the shift of population to areas beyond the city boundaries. The economic standing of the city dramatically changed too, although throughout the war Leeds proved itself to be of great importance, with its factories producing large quantities of artillery, guns, tanks and clothing. Immediately after the war the first signs of decline in the city's manufacturing output were seen.

Between the wars there were very high levels of unemployment brought about by foreign competition and falling world trade. The pride of Leeds and its engineering industry was hit hard. The General Strike of 1926 saw the people of Leeds, often in large numbers, involved in riots with some serious clashes. The one industry that did seem to scrape through all this, against all odds, was clothing. Tailoring shops such as Hepworths had opened up a chain of shops. But the most influential figure here was Montague Burton, a Jewish immigrant who

in 1909 opened his first factory. By 1914 Leeds had become the centre of his operation specializing in the manufacture and selling of suits. His main aim was to make buying a ready-made suit less of an inconvenience than made-to-measure. He could produce a suit quicker and cheaper without any great loss in quality. In 1921 he transferred all his production to a new factory in Hudson Road and by 1925 it was the largest clothing factory in Europe. The Burton chain of tailoring shops grew rapidly in all parts of England and by 1939 there were 595 of them. Another Leeds tailoring firm to become a household name was John Collins. There was such a huge demand for workers, especially female, that when local sources of labour became exhausted other factories had to be built, especially over the Pennines in Lancashire.

The 1930s saw the beginning of a Leeds icon known throughout the world and one that the city would rather forget. The notorious slums had been cleared and in its place the Quarry Hill Flats were built, the first stage opening in March 1938. The model for this new kind of housing estate had been taken from Vienna's Karl Marx Hof, consisting of monumental flats, with formal courtyards and gardens. Sadly the proposed tennis courts and bowling green were never built. The aim was to rehouse those who had originally been temporally relocated when the slums were cleared. However, for whatever reason new residents were reluctant to move, possibly preferring to stay where they were, not too far off the ground. Structural defects and the failure of a revolutionary system of transporting

ABOVE LEFT
Quarry House

LEFT
View of St Peter's Church

West Yorkshire Playhouse

the domestic refuse direct from the flats to the city incinerators led to the demolition of the flats forty years later. The site of Quarry Hill has had a very colourful historical story: the site of a prehistoric camp, a Roman fort, an isolation settlement for plague victims, a Victorian slum which was home to 9,000 people and probably even more rats and a block of flats, a little ahead of its time, where nobody wanted to live. Today there is Quarry House, once again shrouded in controversy, built in 1993 to house the Department of Health and Social Security.

During the Second World War Leeds was hit by nine raids, the worst of which occurred on the night of 14/15 March 1941, in which there was extensive damage to the city centre and many of the public buildings were hit. Compared to other cities Leeds escaped relatively lightly. The city's traditional industries played a vital part in the war effort. Armoured fighting vehicles, including tanks, were produced in vast numbers as well as shells and gun and mortar barrels, and of course uniforms: a

44

Henry Moore Institute

7 February –
4 May 2008

Admission Free

Victoria Quarter, Briggate

Harvey Nichols, Briggate

quarter of all the uniforms required by the Army, Navy and Air Force were produced by Montague Burton.

The post-war years saw no significant growth in Leeds. The textile and engineering industries ticked over while service industries such as gas, electric and water did grow, along with insurance and banking. Losses in one counterweighted gains in others. In the 1960s and 1970s the BBC set up studios in Woodhouse Lane, as did Yorkshire Television in Kirkstall Road. Today the largest employers in Leeds are probably public utilities, health, insurance and banking. Employment in manufacturing has noticeably declined.

During the 1980s and 1990s the city continued to prosper economically. Printing, a field in which Leeds was doing particularly well, had its largest centre outside London. Architecturally the 1980s saw the beginning of the so called 'Leeds Look', which was an attempt to restore the visual appearance of the

ABOVE
City Square

LEFT
No. 1 City Square

Brewery Wharf

city centre using traditional materials, in a modern idiom, in a historic setting. Examples include the Henry Moore Institute (1980–2) and the West Yorkshire Playhouse (1985–90), being somewhat dwarfed by Quarry House in 1993. The Leeds Development Corporation was established in 1987 to revive areas affected by industrial decline. Its first aim was the regeneration of the disused waterfront along the canal and River Aire. Some developments were more successful than others. The transformation of listed warehouses, combined with the new build of The Calls in 1987, was extremely well received, while the Asda offices not quite so much. As in Manchester and Bristol, the intention was to build a residential district around a tourist attraction and thoughts turned to how to go forward with Clarence Dock. This came in the shape of the Royal Armouries, completed in 1996, which houses the collections previously displayed at the Tower of London. Work continued along the

riverside and canal with redevelopments and conversions of warehouses into residential use and offices.

Plans were also afoot to redevelop the city centre as a major shopping area. New life was brought to Thornton's Arcade, Queens Arcade, City Markets and the Corn Exchange. The most outstanding achievement at this time was the refurbishment of the County and Cross Arcades; the shop fronts were restored to their original brilliance and further enhanced by installing a roof canopy over Victoria Street. By so doing the rather splendid Victoria Quarter was complete, housing today many fine shops, including Harvey Nichols.

Interest in traditional architectural forms and materials was beginning to falter and this is shown particularly in the city's next major development: No. 1 City Square (1996–8), a post-modern building with a glass elevator running right up the middle. Since the turn of the century, the trend has been

ABOVE
Granary Wharf

RIGHT
Clarence Dock

ABOVE
Granary Wharf

LEFT
No. 1 Whitehall riverside

LEFT
Clarence Dock

RIGHT ABOVE
Royal Armouries

RIGHT
Clarence Bridge and Royal Armouries

towards residential and mixed-use developments, particularly along the riverside and canal and on a grand scale at Clarence Dock. Butlers Wharf, with its restaurants and hotels, is a great success. Work is ongoing at Granary Wharf, most of which will consist of new buildings. Further along the river there is and will be a whole mass of new high-rise buildings. Much of the 'not quite so good to look at' architecture of Leeds of the 1960s and 1970s has now either been re-clad or demolished. Leeds is a city of varieties with a buoyant economy and planners and architects who wish to continue developing its character.

RIGHT
Aire Street

RIGHT BELOW
View from Beggars Hill

FAR RIGHT
City Markets, Kirkgate

the city

ABOVE
View of Leeds and St Anne's
Cathedral

LEFT
View of The Queens Hotel

ABOVE
View of Headrow and Victoria
Gardens

RIGHT
City view

OVERLEAF
View of Leeds and St Paul's House

LEFT
Park Row

ABOVE
Greek Street

LEFT AND RIGHT
Princess Exchange, Aire Street

LEFT ABOVE
City Markets, Vicar Lane

LEFT
City Markets

RIGHT
Quebec Street

LEFT
Princess Exchange, Princess
Square

ABOVE
City Square

LEFT
The Bourse, Boar Lane

FAR LEFT ABOVE
Bibis Restaurant

FAR LEFT BELOW
Malmaison, Concordia Street

arcades and markets

There are four shopping arcades in Leeds which are un-matched anywhere. They were all built in the Victorian era when there was a desire for structures where shoppers could pursue their pastime sheltered from the elements. With new materials just becoming available, especially the invention of plate glass, it was possible to have large shop fronts where the keepers could show their goods, replacing the windows formed from little panes of glass in the traditional Georgian shop. Window shopping had arrived. The first to be built was Thornton's Arcade (1877–8), in which there is a particularly fine clock with cast-iron figures by a local firm of William Potts & Sons. Queens Arcade (1889) was the next. But the two main

OPPOSITE AND BELOW
Queens Arcade

arcades are County and Cross Arcades, by Frank Matcham, were the last to be built in 1898–1904. They are in total contrast to the notorious slums that had previously occupied this site. They were the most opulent arcades in England, top lit by a glass barrel-vaulted roof, highly decorated using marble and mosaics and with shop fronts made from mahogany. There are impressive entrances to the Victoria Quarter from both the Briggate and the Vicar Lane ends.

At around the same time in 1904 the Corporation was building the new City Markets on the same site as the long-established Kirkgate Market, which had opened in 1822 to

house Briggate's fruit and vegetable traders. The design of the new market hall, the winner of a competition, was by Leeming & Leeming, who had previously been the architects of Halifax Market Hall, which had opened in 1898. Their latest venture was to be on a grander scale with a skyline of domes and pinnacles under which was to be a magnificent market hall, largely made up of glass and cast iron built in the Flemish style with Art Nouveau detailing.

BELOW LEFT AND RIGHT
City Markets, Kirkgate

clocks

Clocks and time seem to have played a very important role in the lives of the citizens of Leeds in the Victorian era and the firm of William Potts & Sons were a large part in it. William Potts 1804–87 was the son of a Darlington clockmaker and he began learning the art of clock making from a very early age. William set up business in Pudsey in 1833 specializing in large clocks. Much of his work can still be seen today at various locations throughout the city: the clock at Leeds Town Hall, which he designed in 1860, The Griffin Hotel in Boar Lane in 1877, and at Thornton's Arcade off Briggate in 1878, with its mechanical figures of Ivanhoe, Robin Hood, Friar Tuck and Richard the Lionheart. In the Grand Arcade off Vicar Lane there is a similar timepiece from 1897, which has two guardsmen. There is also a very unusual clock on the front of the jewellery shop of James Dyson in Lower Briggate. A very different one is situated at the entrance to Roudhay Park which is free standing and originally stood in the City Markets before being moved in 1912.

RIGHT
William Potts clock, Roundhay Park

FAR RIGHT ABOVE
William Potts clock, Grand Arcade

FAR RIGHT BELOW
William Potts clock, Thornton's Arcade

music halls and theatres

LEFT AND BELOW
City Varieties Music Hall, Swan Street

On 7 June 1851 Thornton's New Music Hall and Fashionable Lounge saw its opening night. It had come into being after Charles Thornton had built onto one of his rooms at The White Swan Inn, in Swan Street. It was the beginning of a trend that was to grow in popularity. As competition grew Thornton decided to change his business interests and put his money into property, building Thornton's Arcade next door to the Music Hall. The City Varieties Music Hall continued under various owners and still survives today.

The Grand Theatre in Upper Briggate was built in 1877–8 by George Corson, greatly influenced by his assistant James Robertson Watson, who had undertaken a tour of European churches and theatres. It possesses an interior which, like the Music Hall, has changed very little. Only the owners of the tickets for best seats were allowed to use the main entrance, while the owners of the cheaper ones had to use the side doors and a labyrinth of staircases and passages to get to their seats. The comfort of the seats also varied according to the price paid for the ticket: either plush and soft upholstery or a wooden bench. Luckily today all the seating is of the soft upholstered kind, but the maze of stairs and passages still exists along with the magnificent decoration especially in the auditorium.

Leeds' third theatre, in total contrast to the other two, is the West Yorkshire Playhouse. It is a modern theatre, built along with Quarry House, the College of Music and the BBC studios in an attempt to rejuvenate an area that had had a long and historic past. Quarry Hill Flats, which had previously occupied the site, had been demolished in 1978. The Playhouse, next to Quarry House, was built in 1985–90, but its attempt at the 'Leeds Look' was not quite as successful and exciting as the interior, which dramatically makes use of exposed girders and beams to give it an almost industrial appearance. It is made up of two separate theatres: the larger Quarry Theatre which has a capacity of 750 and the more intimate Courtyard Theatre which seats 350.

The Grand Theatre, Upper Briggate

The Quarry Theatre, West Yorkshire
Playhouse

churches

St John the Baptist, Adel

Although not within the city boundaries, St John the Baptist is worthy of inclusion as it contains some very distinguished and rare Norman decorative work. The key features include the chancel arch and the doorway arch. (Sadly the exceptionally fine Norman bronze door ring made in York around 1200 was stolen in 2002 and the one seen today is a replica.) The building itself dates back to between 1150 and 1170, although there has been some restoration work. The bellcote and rebuilding of the west gable was carried out by R.D. Chantrell in 1838. Other work including the chancel roof and further interior restoration work was undertaken by G.E. Street in 1878–9 when the box pews were removed.

ABOVE AND RIGHT
St John the Baptist, Adel

St John the Evangelist, New Briggate

St John the Evangelist was built in 1631 and was founded by the very wealthy wool merchant John Harrison. It is the oldest surviving church in Leeds and a rarity in that it has remained virtually intact. It did have a close call in the mid-nineteenth century when, as was quite often the case during the Victorian era, there were calls for its restoration and even demolition, as it was thought that St John's was old fashioned. Luckily demolition was ruled out and what restoration that did take place in 1866 was mostly undone in 1885. The great glory of St Johns is the Jacobean woodwork, particularly the screen, which bears the coat of arms of James I on its north side and Charles I on its south, which was probably the work of Francis Gunby.

St John the Evangelist, New
Briggate

St Peter, Kirkgate

St Peter's was built in 1837–41 by R.D. Chantrell. It is affectionally known as the Parish Church as it was denied cathedral status in the late nineteenth century. Dr Walter Farquhar Hook, Vicar of Leeds for twenty-two years, was responsible, along with Chantrell, for the St Peter's we see today. It replaced the original medieval church with a spacious, open church, in great contrast to the clutter of the old one. Dr Hook's personal appeal attracted very large congregations and he was passionately interested in the education of the young, especially those from poor backgrounds. Of course around this time children were working extremely long hours in the mills and factories and at every possible opportunity Dr Hook reminded the mill and factory owners, many of whom happened to be his parishioners, of their duties to those who could not help themselves. He proved to be a very influential figure: when he arrived in Leeds there were only eight churches and during his time here the number increased to thirty-six. He even had time to urge the town council to purchase Woodhouse Moor and convert it to a public park.

St Bartholomew, Armley

At the top of Wesley Road, the highest point in Armley and visible from all over the city, stands St Bartholomew's, built in 1872–8 by Henry Walker and Joseph Athron. Very little is known about them except that this church was their only large-scale work. And it is colossal. This lofty interior houses an organ case of huge proportions also by Walker and Athron, which in turn houses the celebrated organ by J.F. Schulze.

St Saviour, Ellerby Road

St Saviour's was built in 1842–5 by John Macduff Derick, an Irishman from County Sligo. It is possibly the most important Victorian Church in Leeds, mainly due to its stained-glass windows. The west window, along with the north and south transept windows, are by A.W.N. Pugin. The east window was designed by Michael O'Conner, while other windows in the nave are by the Pre-Raphaelite artists William Morris, Ford Maddox-Brown and Edward Burne-Jones. The chancel screen and the reredos are by B.F. Bodley. The interior has undergone four major refurbishments, the first by G.E. Street in 1866–7, the second in 1885–90 by B.F. Bodley, a third by George Pace in 1963 and finally in 2006–8, when the nineteenth-century decorations were reinstated and the 1960s paintwork removed.

St Hilda, Cross Green Lane

St Hilda's was built in 1876–82 by J.T. Micklethwaite, who believed 'as money is scarce the outside of the church shall be perfectly plain and we will concentrate on making the interior as beautiful as possible'. The painted wooden furnishings by W.H. Wood of Newcastle in the Gothic style were not installed until the twentieth century and the magnificent rood screen in 1922–3. The pulpit of 1882 was decorated to match the screen.

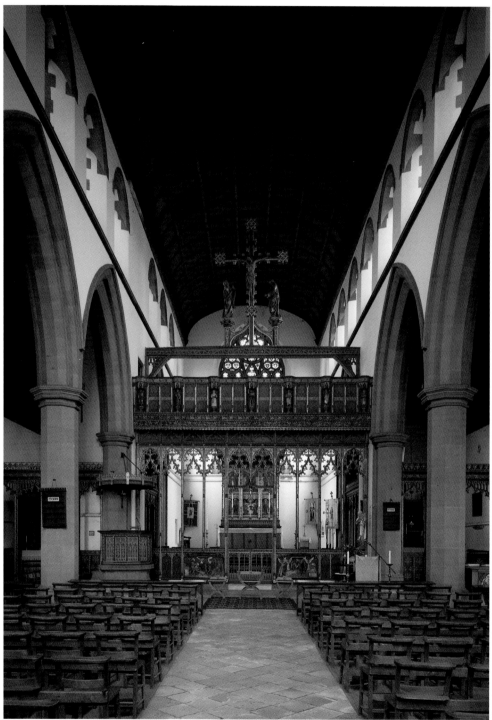

St Aiden, Roundhay Road

St Aiden's was built to serve this working class district at the request of Dr Jayne, Vicar of Leeds in 1889 to the designs of R.L. Johnson and A. Crawford Hick of Newcastle. Its style seems to draw upon influences from all over Europe. Sadly Johnson who had entered the competition for the design of the church died within months of it being accepted and much of the detail work was done by Crawford. The particularly fine mosaics in the chancel are by Sir Frank Brangwyn.

ABOVE AND RIGHT
St Aiden, Roundhay Road

St Martin, Chapeltown Road

St Martin's was built in 1879–81 by Adams and Kelly. It is another of those churches where the visitor receives a very unexpected surprise. Never underestimate what riches lie within from what may appear to be a rather plain exterior. The whole of the chancel walls are covered with splendid murals completed by Hemming & Co. in 1913. The equally colourful reredos of carved gilded wood replaced the original stone one some time between 1898 and 1905.

ABOVE AND RIGHT
St Martin, Chapeltown Road

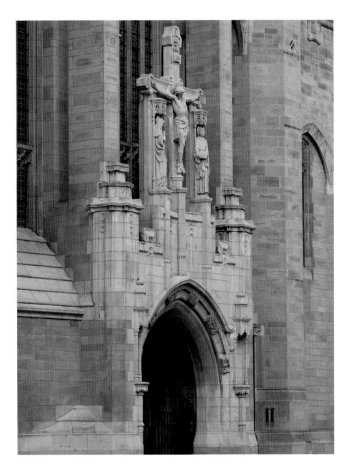

St Anne's Cathedral, Cookridge Street

The relatively modern Roman Catholic church of St Anne's is Leeds' only cathedral. The architect was J.H. Eastwood and it was built by William Cowling and Sons in 1901–4 in the gothic Art & Crafts style. It replaced the old St Anne's church built in 1883, which stood on the opposite side of Cookridge Street and was demolished in 1901 in order to widen the road.

ABOVE AND RIGHT
St Anne's Cathedral, Cookridge
Street

leeds town hall

Leeds Town Hall was built in 1852–8 by Cuthbert Brodrick and is without doubt one of the most spectacular buildings of its kind in the country. In 1851 a group of Leeds citizens had foundered the Leeds Improvement Society, who believed their duty was 'to erect a noble municipal palace in their squalid and unbeautiful town'. Strong words, but they meant what they said. Within a year, land for the new building had been purchased. It was decided, as was quite often the case, to open an architectural competition. Sixteen designs were entered and the one by Brodrick, a thirty-year-old man from Hull was chosen as the winning entry. The brief for the proposed building which had been sent to all the contestants stated that it should contain a hall capable of seating 8,000 people, room for an orchestra and a balcony, a mayoral suite, a Council Chamber, four courtrooms and accommodation for council offices and the police. Leeds did indeed want a municipal palace.

The original design by Brodrick was very much influenced by his travels abroad and its style derived from buildings he had seen in Paris. The amount of money allocated for the proposed building was not huge (a leading factor as to why there had been so few entries for its design in the first place). However it was at a time when Leeds was campaigning to be appointed the West Riding Assize town in opposition to Wakefield and Sheffield, neither of which could boast of a building quite like the proposed Leeds Town Hall. Fairly quickly the original budget was abandoned and designs changed but the French Neoclassical flavour remained.

It was not until 1853 that a decision was made to build a tower. The original design for it did not meet with everyone's approval and in 1854 Brodrick submitted a watercolour painting of how he felt the tower should look. This design was accepted and work was started on the foundations, which involved a considerable amount of work and much revision to the designs for the rest of the building. By 1856 there was generally a growing pride in the building of what was 'to show the wealth and importance of the town'. Subtle embellishments were made and the original budget of £35,000 was soon forgotten.

Today Leeds Town Hall sits in a very commanding position. From wherever you are in the city, from whichever angle, it says exactly what it set out to say. It is approached by a broad, monumental flight of steps, guarded by four lions made from Portland stone. There is a set of huge doors, above which is a sculptured tympanum by John Thomas. Through these doors the visitor enters the vestibule with its floor of Minton tiles, its lavish decoration and stunning ceiling giving a flavour of what is to come. Immediately in front is the Victoria Hall, which offers everything the Victorian period had to offer in terms of decoration. The colours and vastness are quite breathtaking, with every surface either gilded or painted. It was work of a fashionable London decorator of the time, John Crace.

The Victoria Hall has survived relatively unchanged and still regularly hosts concerts as was intended. Other rooms within the Town Hall have changed as modern times have demanded and as a civic building it continues to serve the needs of the people of Leeds.

LEFT
Vestibule ceiling, Town Hall

ABOVE
Town Hall

LEFT AND RIGHT
Victoria Hall, Town Hall

the civic hall

The Civic Hall was built in 1931–3 to the designs of E. Vincent Harris, who was also responsible for similar public buildings in Manchester and Sheffield. It is situated at the top of the sloping, recently renamed Millenium Square, giving it a very graceful position. It is Palladian in style and the main south-facing portico is supported by four giant Corinthian columns.

the corn exchange

With the success of Leeds Town Hall behind him, Cuthbert Brodrick submitted an entry for the proposed new Corn Exchange. The old one in Briggate, built only thirty years previously, had been deemed unsuitable by the merchants of Leeds. A new one was needed and a site had been chosen next to the White Cloth Hall and Kirkgate Market. Many believe its design to be Brodrick's finest work, possessing as it does the unusual stonework, inspired again by his travels abroad, this time not only France, but Italy as well, which is probably where his idea for the diamond rusticated stonework originated. The huge domed roof of the interior is made from a mixture of wrought iron, cast iron and timber, with a glazed panel on the north side to let in natural light. The ironwork was carried out by Butler & Co., the successors to the Kirkstall Forge.

LEFT AND RIGHT
The Corn Exchange

LEFT AND RIGHT
The Corn Exchange

the university of leeds

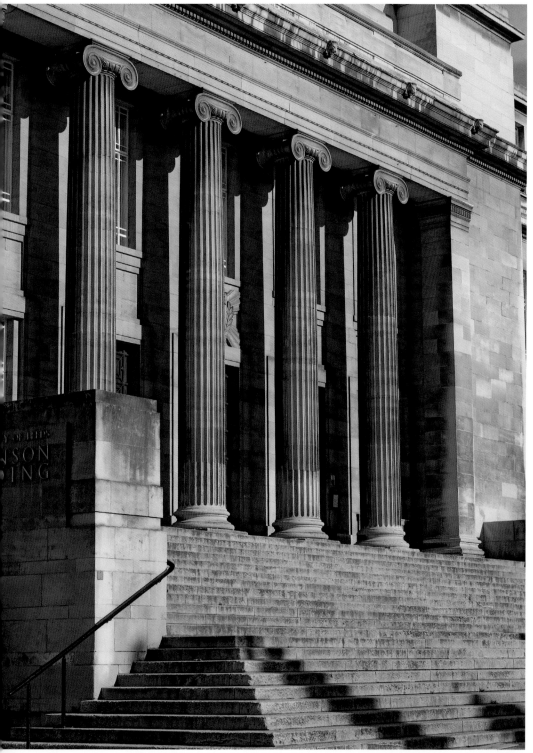

Parkinson Building, Woodhouse
Lane

The University of Leeds started out as the Yorkshire College of Science, which was founded in 1874. Today the campus of the University is spread over a large area, not only with buildings that were purpose-built but also incorporating numerous early-nineteenth-century terraces and villas that have survived and been adapted for residential and teaching purposes. The other main buildings within the campus are of three distinctive styles and are as varied in style as they are in the materials used.

The first architect to be appointed was Alfred Waterhouse, who in 1877 was asked to draw up plans for the School of Textile and Design. There had been an attempted fund raising which had raised £20,000 out of a hoped-for £60,000. Luckily the shortfall was made up by the Clothworkers Company of London and the building completed by 1879. The Baines Wing, again by Waterhouse was built in 1881–5, named after Sir Edward Baines, Chairman of the College Council. Between these two buildings the Great Hall was inserted in 1890–4. Alfred's son Paul added extensions to both the Baines Wing in 1908 and the Textiles Wing in 1909–12, again paid for by the Clothworkers. The Agricultural Building, now the Geography Building, was built by Paul's son Michael Waterhouse in 1923–5.

The second style came a little later in the 1930s, when plans submitted by Lancaster, Lucas and Lodge were chosen to build a new library. Edward Brotherton gave £100,000 towards the costs and on his death his private collection of books, which was duly donated in 1935, one year before the Brotherton Library was opened. The intention was for the library to sit behind a central administration block with an entrance to the street. This came in 1936 when Frank Parkinson gave £200,000 towards the construction of the new building, in which the Brotherton is located today. The Parkinson Building is a monumental east-facing building made from Portland stone, with a grand staircase and a landmark clock tower, which all sit in a very commanding position at the top of a rise out of the city centre.

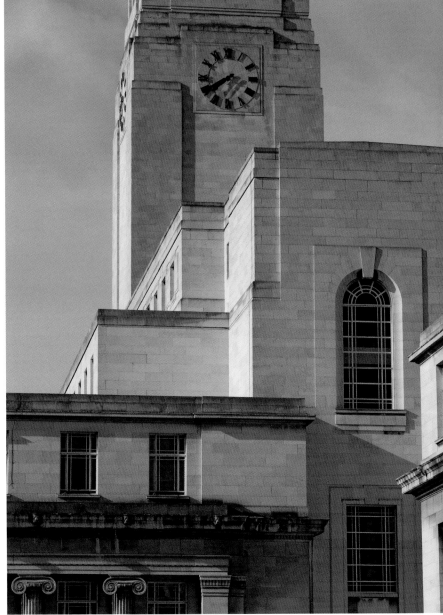

The third style of architecture was even more diverse than the previous two. In 1959, Chamberlin, Powell and Bon were appointed to undertake a number of new buildings within the campus. An extensive survey was done to estimate the university's future needs and of the increase in student numbers. Eventually a plan was drawn up. The buildings were all made from concrete blocks, which were clad and later painted. The main buildings were grouped around the Chancellors Court, the centrepiece of which was the Roger Stevens Building (1968–70).

ABOVE LEFT
Great Hall and Parkinson Building
clock tower

ABOVE
Baines Wing and School of Textiles
and Design

RIGHT ABOVE
Baines Wing and Great Hall

RIGHT
The School of Geography

FAR LEFT, ABOVE
The School of Mathematics

FAR LEFT, BELOW
The Roger Stevens Building

LEFT
The Brotherton Library

roundhay park

The land on which Roundhay Park is situated today is first mentioned in an 1155 charter as the deer park of the de Lacy family. Through marriage between Alice de Lacy and the Earl of Lancaster it passed to the future Henry IV, becoming land of the Crown, as part of it still remains today. The rest passed through various hands until the estate was auctioned in 1871, when Sir John Barran, the Lord Mayor of Leeds and a number of colleagues acquired it for use as a public park.

A competition was held for the landscaping of the estate in order to make it suitable for day-trippers. It was won by George Corson, but his ideas for the development were slow to take form. The problem was that the park was too far from the city and it wasn't until the introduction of the tramway in 1891 that the park began to really enjoy great success.

The Rotunda, a classical domed drinking fountain, was designed by Thomas Ambler and was paid for by John Barran in 1882, a working partnership which had been responsible for the building of St Paul's House in Park Square four years earlier.

Around the outskirts of the park there are today a mixture houses and villas in various styles, many built around 1900 and all very smart, making the area as a whole, a very respectable part of residential Leeds.

LEFT AND BELOW
The Rotunda, Roundhay Park

kirkstall abbey

Kirkstall Abbey is the oldest medieval building in Leeds. It was founded by a group of Cistercian monks who moved away from Fountains Abbey. After settling for short time at Barnoldswick in 1147, they moved again in 1152 to a site in the Aire valley which they called Kirkstall. The original abbey was probably built from wood but the grit stone abbey we see today, paid for by their patron Henry de Lacy, dates from 1182. The abbey had vast estates with farms managed by the lay brothers. They reared sheep, traded in wool and were the instigators of the vast industry and wealth that befell Leeds in the future. The site on which the abbey stands originally consisted of a church and monastic buildings built around a cloister. Some of the buildings remain remarkably intact, while others, such as the infirmary, were lost completely the foundations of which were discovered in 1893, during work carried out by Leeds City Corporation who were developing the abbey precincts into a public park.

LEFT AND FAR LEFT
Kirkstall Abbey

temple newsam

Temple Newsam sits in all its grandeur across a sea of green in a landscape by Lancelot 'Capability' Brown. This great Jacobean house is only 4 miles from Leeds and has evolved over five centuries.

The manor of Newsam was first mentioned in the Domesday Book in 1086. In 1155 it became the property of the Knights Templar and on their suppression in the early fourteenth century it passed into the family of Thomas, Lord Darcy, who between 1488 and 1521 built a house on the present site. (In 1537 he was executed for treason.) In 1622 it was acquired by Sir Arthur Ingram who rebuilt the house incorporating Darcy's west wing. The work that was carried out transformed it into a great house of the Jacobean period. Between 1736 and 1746, Henry Ingram, Sir Arthur's son, remodelled the north and west wings. A number of architects were consulted during this period of work on the house, one being John Carr of York. It was at this time or a little later, perhaps in the 1760s, that the grounds were landscaped by 'Capability' Brown. In 1820 the drawing room was decorated with the very distinctive Chinese wallpaper, a gift from the Prince Regent to Lady Hertford who had inherited the house in 1807. Towards the end of the nineteenth century further work was carried out, chiefly by C.E. Kempe, which included the oak staircase of 1894.

In 1909 the estate was compulsory purchased by Leeds Corporation in order to build a sewage plant. The house remained in the Ingram family until 1922, when it was sold by a descendant, Edward Wood, 1st Earl of Halifax, to Leeds Corporation for a nominal sum without its contents. During the Second World War Leeds Corporation temporarily moved the main collection of the City Art Gallery to the house for safety and it was during this period that the decoration was sadly neglected. Since 1983 a programme of restoration and redecoration has been carried out in an attempt to return this wonderful example to its former glory, gradually filling it with furniture that has a direct provenance to Temple Newsam. This has been successfully achieved by Anthony Wells-Cole and his predecessor.

BELOW
Temple Newsam House

RIGHT
Staircase, Temple Newsam

headingley cricket ground

In 1890 The Leeds Cricket, Football and Athletic Company was formed at a ground in Headingley. It was the only sports ground in the area so it attracted other sports, including lawn tennis, bowls, rugby and cycling. The first cricket match played at the new ground was in May 1890 between Leeds and Scarborough. Yorkshire played their first county match against Derbyshire in June 1891. The ground played host to its first Test Match when England took on Australia for the Ashes in June 1899, which England lost. England's first victory at Headingley was against South Africa in 1907. Headingley soon became an institution with the cricket-going public and still remains as such today. Many cricketing highlights have taken place here, including the Australian Donald Bradman scoring triple centuries in 1930 and 1934 and England's famous victory led by Ian Botham over the Australians in 1981. The Headingley Carnegie Stadium as it is called today plays host to both Yorkshire County Cricket Club and the Leeds Rugby League Club, Leeds Rhinos. The two grounds sit next to each other and are separated by a dual serving stand. Both grounds have undergone extensive re-development over recent years.

LEFT AND RIGHT
Headingley Cricket Ground

river aire

ABOVE
Whitehall II

LEFT AND RIGHT
Whitehall waterfront

Bridgewater Place

Granary Wharf

ABOVE LEFT
Tower Works and Bridgewater Place

ABOVE RIGHT
Bridgewater Place

BELOW LEFT
No. 1 Whitehall riverside and
Whitehall Bridge

BELOW RIGHT
Whitehall waterfront

index